Artists at Work
Wood

Cheryl Jakab

A⁺

Smart Apple Media

Smart Apple Media
2140 Howard Drive West
North Mankato
Minnesota 56003

First published in 2006 by
MACMILLAN EDUCATION AUSTRALIA PTY LTD
627 Chapel Street, South Yarra, Australia 3141

Visit our Web site at www.macmillan.com.au

Associated companies and representatives throughout the world.

Copyright © Cheryl Jakab 2006

Library of Congress Cataloging-in-Publication Data

Jakab, Cheryl.
   Wood / by Cheryl Jakab.
   p. cm.—Artists at work)
   Includes index.
   ISBN-13: 978-1-58340-776-9
   1. Woodwork—Juvenile literature. I. Title.

   NK9604.2.J25 2006
   684'.08—dc22   2005056774

Edited by Sam Munday
Text and cover design by Karen Young
Page layout by Karen Young
Photo research by Jes Senbergs
Illustrations by Ann Likhovetsky

Printed in USA

Acknowledgments

The author would like to acknowledge and thank all the working artists and hobbyists who have been quoted, appear, or assisted in creating this book.

The author and the publisher are grateful to the following for permission to reproduce copyright material:

Cover photograph: Maestro Bissolotti closing the case of a violin at his studio in Cremona, Italy, courtesy of David Lees/CORBIS.

Wedding Chapel IV, 1960 (painted wood), Nevelson, Louise (1900-88)/Private Collection/Bridgeman Art Library, p. 11; Coo-ee Picture Library, p. 26; Corbis, pp. 4 (bottom right), 7, 10, 12, 13, 14, 15, 16 (both), 18, 19, 21; Rob Cruse, pp. 9 (top), 9 (middle), 25; Istock, p. 4 (top); Cheryl Jakab, p. 5; Lebrecht Arts & Music Picture Library, p. 17 (both); Lonely Planet Images, p. 9 (bottom); Photodisc, p. 6; Photolibrary.com, p. 20; STAX, DIDGEMAN, www.didgeman.com.au, p. 22; http://www.woodturningcenter.org, website design: Galactic Graphics c.1995-2005, p. 24; www.wasteconverters.com.au, p. 27; Vic Wood, pp. 4 (bottom left), 23.

While every care has been taken to trace and acknowledge copyright, the publisher tenders their apologies for any accidental infringement where copyright has proved untraceable. Where the attempt has been unsuccessful, the publisher welcomes information that would redress the situation.

Please note
At the time of printing, the Internet addresses appearing in this book were correct. Owing to the dynamic nature of the Internet, however, we cannot guarantee that all these addresses will remain correct.

Contents

Glossary words

When a word is printed in **bold**, you can look up its meaning in the Glossary on page 31.

Wood artists

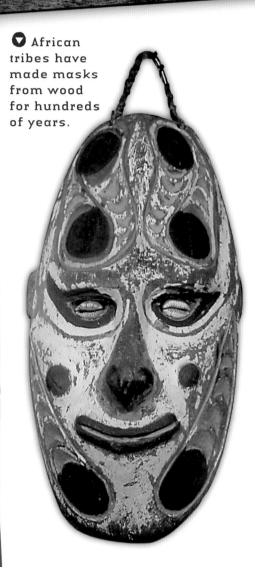

▼ African tribes have made masks from wood for hundreds of years.

Look at these different artworks made by wood artists. Wood artists are people who design and make artworks with wood. Wood artists make a wide variety of items using a range of timbers, including:

- ▶ hand-crafted furniture
- ▶ totem poles
- ▶ masks and statues
- ▶ useful and decorative cups, bowls, and plates
- ▶ musical instruments such as violins and guitars
- ▶ carvings on wall panels, chariots, and boats

▼ Totem poles are carved from one long piece of timber.

▼ Wood artwork can be polished so that it is smooth to the touch.

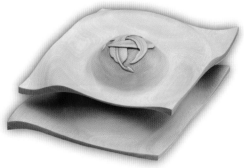

🔺 This wooden bowl, made by wood hobbyist Marion Williams, shows the texture of the wood used.

Using wood

Wood artists are people who are very skilled at shaping or joining selected pieces of wood. In this book, you will find the answers to these questions and more:

▶ What does a wood artist do?

▶ What do wood artists need to know about wood to use it creatively?

▶ How does wood help the artist express their ideas?

▶ What is it that artists like about wood as a **medium** for their art?

"I love the detailed patterns you find inside large tree burls [a type of growth found on tree trunks]. I cut then polish burls with power tools and by hand to a glossy finish."
Marion Williams, schoolteacher and wood hobbyist

What is wood?

Wood is any of the hard parts from a tree. Wood includes the trunk, branches, stems, or the veins in leaves. Even nuts and seed pods can be described as wood. Wood from different types of tree vary in pattern, color, density, and hardness. There are as many varieties of wood as there are of tree.

⬇ Some trees add one growth ring each year.

Patterns in wood

Growth rings and knots create patterns in wood. As a tree grows it becomes thicker. It does this by laying down new wood on the outer edge of the trunk and branches. This growth creates rings.

Knots in wood are areas where the trunk has grown around a branch. When the wood is cut, the knot can be seen as an irregular pattern in the **grain**. Knots create interesting patterns and color in wood.

Softwood and hardwood

Wood can be either softwood or hardwood. "Hardwood" comes from broad-leaved trees, such as oak, eucalypts, and mahogany. "Softwood" comes from trees with needle-like leaves, such as pine, casuarina, and spruce. Hardwoods have a fine grain appearance. Softwoods usually have a similar surface to each other and often have a great deal of resin in them.

Woods have their own textures, colors, and fragrances. Wood artists use different woods for different purposes.

Common woods

Hardwoods	Examples	Tree description	Characteristics	Uses
	oak	large tree from the beech family with acorn fruits	• very hard wearing • fine-grained	• barrel making • veneers • flooring • bridge girders • paneling
	mahogany	tropical tree found in Africa and America	• dark-reddish color • strong • heavy • easily worked	• furniture • building materials (before the largest trees were all cut down)
	blackwood	large tree that grows in Eastern Australia	• golden brown to reddish brown with dark streaks • very hard	• furniture
Softwoods	pine	evergreen tree which can be fast-growing	• pale-yellow color • grainy	• building materials or furniture (depends on species)
	cedar	evergreen tree with a red trunk	• red-colored • hard wearing • fragrant	• cabinet making • pencils • building materials

Wood work

Wood artists make use of the different characteristics of wood in their work. They try to give their works beauty using the natural variety of colors, textures, and grain in wood.

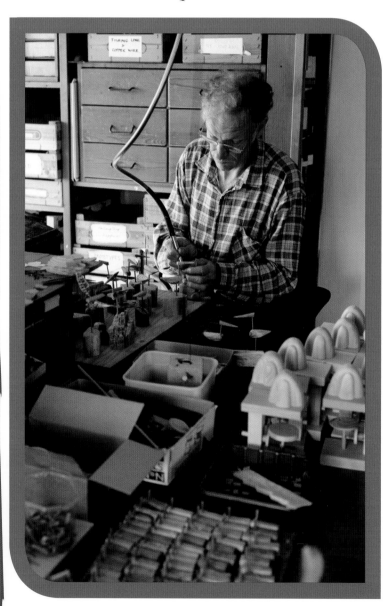

Some wood artworks are small and very detailed.

Wood artists often become skilled in one or two techniques while working with different types of wood. Different techniques require different tools. Wood working techniques include:

- general carpentry such as sawing, drilling, and planing
- expert carving with chisels, **augers**, and sandpaper
- turning wood on a **lathe**
- joining, such as **tongue and groove** joins
- expert finishing, including polishing and **laminating**

Creating with wood

Work in wood is direct, once a cut has been made in wood it cannot be unmade. The way wood has grown affects the timber, so each piece is different. The artist needs to work with these differences when creating with wood.

Advantages of working with wood

The advantages of working with wood are that it:

- is light, strong, and flexible
- comes in a great variety of colors and textures
- is easily cut and joined
- can be bent into shape
- can be colored with stains and paints
- can be polished to a smooth finish

 **The Artist Speaks**

"Wood is organic and unpredictable. The way it has grown and the structure of the plant are recorded in the wood."
Steve Horton, wood turner

▼ ▲ Wood artists can create just about anything with wood.

"King Billy Pine is, in my humble opinion, one of the finest soundboard timbers that grows upon this earth."
Peter Coomb, mandolin maker

▼ Making string instruments is a skill that takes years to learn.

Wood artists today

Many wood artists express their ideas using both traditional and new techniques. New ideas can develop as a trend and are adopted by other artists or even used in mass-produced items.

Changes in working with wood

Wood artists are discovering new timbers to explore using traditional techniques. The technique for making string instruments has not changed for hundreds of years. The sound a violin or mandolin makes can change depending on the type of wood it is made from. The front of the violin is usually made of **well-seasoned** spruce and the back is made of maple. Some of the best violins being made today are based on traditional designs, but with new timbers.

New techniques

Artists today are still fascinated by the traditional ways of working wood but are also developing new techniques. Power tools for example, make working wood easier. Throughout the 1900s, artists working with wood maintained traditional designs using power saws, lathes, drills, and sanders. Many modern wood sculptures show the grains and textures of the wood.

▶ This sculpture *Wedding Chapel IV*, was created by Louise Nevelson, a Russian-American sculptor.

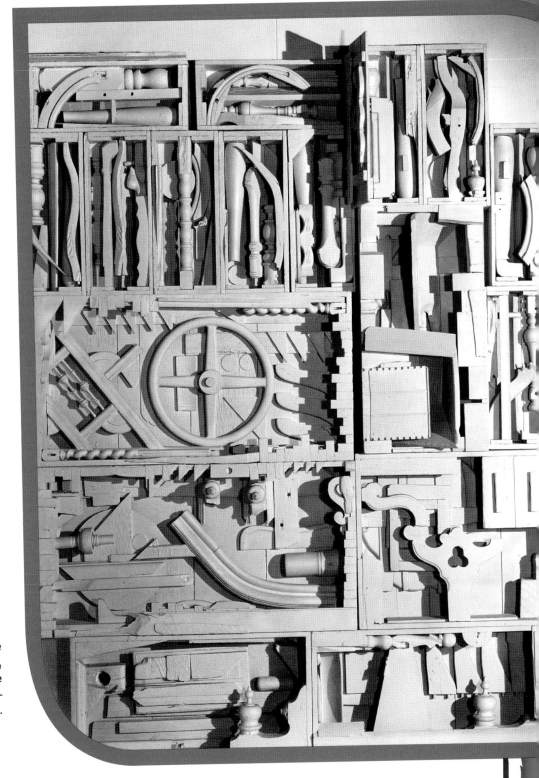

"The grain of wood plays a part [in the sculpture] and makes it alive."
Henry Moore, **English sculptor**

Wood turning

Wood turning is a wood-shaping technique that involves rapidly turning wood against a cutting tool. The machine that turns the wood is called a lathe. Lathes can be used to turn items such as table legs, bowls, and posts.

To turn a piece of wood, the artist mounts the block of wood to the lathe, attaching it with screws at one end. As the lathe turns the piece of wood, the artist presses the cutting tool against it. The artist controls how quickly the lathe turns and the depth and angle of the cutting tool. This allows the artist to shape wood evenly and accurately.

▶ The harder the artist presses, the deeper the tool will cut.

Finishing

After the shape is complete, the artist can then use the lathe to finish the surface of the piece. First they sand the piece by holding a piece of sandpaper against the wood as it turns on the lathe. This achieves a smooth, even surface. The artist then applies a coating such as wax or lacquer while the piece is turning. This ensures that the piece is evenly coated and smooth.

▲ This turned wood is being smoothed with sandpaper.

Wood art history

It is difficult to know when woodwork began as an art form. Much of what has been made from wood in the past has rotted away. Wood was a major material for artwork until the 1800s when metals began to replace wood for many uses.

Tools

Many tools used for working wood today have been used since ancient times. These include saws, chisels, rasps, **planes**, and the wood lathe. The way the lathes are powered has developed greatly through time. The earliest woodworking lathes, powered by rotating a pole, were developed around 600 B.C. These pole lathes were replaced by foot-powered lathes in the 1300s. Lathes were later powered by water, steam, and electricity. Modern lathes work on the same principle as ancient lathes but are capable of more precise shaping and have improved power sources.

◀ The figurehead of this Maori longboat has been carved from wood by using saws and chisels.

Great wood traditions

Some woodworking traditions stand out due to the skill of the artists.

Gothic wood carving

In the 1400s and 1500s in Europe, many of the elaborate furnishings of churches were hand carved out of wood. In France, Germany, and Spain, carved panels of wood told a story and were set in elaborate frames. The Belgian cities of Antwerp, Brussels, and Malines were famous centres for these "retables" and exported them all over Europe. This carved wood was also used to decorate buildings other than churches.

▶ This French gothic staircase at Leeds Castle, England, is carved in oak.

Wood treasures

Over the years, wood artists have created many different pieces. Some are considered to be valuable treasures.

Ceremonial masks

Masks are an example of classic African artwork. Masks are made to be worn in performances. The mask is often part of a costume combining wood with paint and textiles. The mask itself can have a range of meanings depending on local culture.

◄ This ceremonial mask was made in the Ivory Coast, West Africa.

Totem poles

Totem poles mean different things to different groups. In native American culture, they are carved emblems and sometimes show gods and animals. These tall poles, carved from wood, are like a family crest or family tree. Each "totem" on the pole represents a family. Indigenous Australians use totem poles in ceremonies.

◄ Each totem on this native American totem pole looks different due to the use of color.

△ Antonio Stradivari

Stradivari violins

Violins made by Antonio Stradivari between 1700 and 1725 are said to be the finest ever made. His violins are more sought after than those of any other instrument maker. Hundreds of his violins still exist today. Some experts believe the varnish he used was important in creating the great sound they produce. Violin makers are still trying to match the sound of Stradivari violins.

Antonio Stradivari had a long career at the Cremona school of violin makers in Italy. Stradivari worked under the great master Andrea Amanti, who may have been the inventor of the violin. During his career, Stradivari made many changes to the proportions of violins. He was still making instruments when he was in his nineties.

△ Some violins by Stradivari are over 300 years old and are sold for a lot of money.

CASE STUDY
Ancient Egyptian woodcraft

Around 2500 B.C., ancient Egyptian carpenters were experts in creating fine works in wood. Wooden objects were often expensive and available only to the rich. Wood artists were valued workers and were paid very well for their products. Artists carved items such as headrests, caskets, and even make-up boxes for noblemen and women. Artworks were often decorated with carvings of animals such as lions, goats, and snakes. Many wooden items and paintings of woodworking have been preserved in Egyptian tombs. More examples of ancient Egyptian woodworking tools and furniture are still being discovered today.

▶ Many ancient Egyptian wood carvings are kept in museums.

Types of wood in ancient Egypt

Wood was in very short supply in Egypt. Most of the wood had to be imported from other countries.

Wood	Source	Uses
date palm	Nile valley	• roof timbers
acacia	Nile valley	• pegs and dowels for joining
tamarisk	Nile valley	• walking sticks
sycamore fig	Nile valley	• coffins • chests • statues
cedar	Lebanon	• boats • building materials • furniture
ebony	Southern Africa	• furniture • statues

Woodworking tools

Ancient Egyptian woodworkers used various saws, knives, and choppers to carve wood. After carving, stones were used to give the wood a polished finish. Ancient Egyptians also used a type of drill worked by a bowstring (the bow drill). Expert workers used these tools to create products that were highly valued in ancient Egypt.

▼ Tools such as these were once used in ancient Egypt.

19

Where wood artists work

A wood artist's workshop can also be used to store finished artworks.

The wood artist's workshop is sometimes a large shed or garage with space and light. Depending on the type of work they do, the artist may need a wide range of hand or power tools. Many have both. Many types of tools such as saws, chisels, planes, and files are often stored on walls with a special place for each item. Larger tools such as lathes are also kept in the workshop.

A vacuum cleaner or dust extractor is a useful addition to the wood artist's workshop. Wood dust and shavings need to be collected from the work area regularly. Breathing in too much wood dust can be bad for your lungs. Dust can also stick to painted or varnished artworks. Shavings are slippery and can be dangerous to leave on the floor. Most workshops also have a wood storage area where wood can be kept flat and dry.

CASE STUDY
Studio woodwork

Studio woodworking is the crafting of wood by hand. After the invention of power tools in the 1800s, making wooden items by hand declined in popularity. Furniture was being made in factories and much of it was made of metal. During the 1950s, wood artists rediscovered working timber by hand and gave it the name "studio woodwork."

George Nakashima
(1905–1990)

George Nakashima was a well-known studio wood furniture maker who set trends in **contemporary** design. Nakashima was a Japanese–American who first trained as an architect. He worked with the famous American architect Frank Lloyd Wright. Nakashima made limited numbers of original furniture using carefully selected timbers like walnut and cherry.

⬥ George Nakashima with some of his chair and table designs.

showing wood artworks

It is important for wood artists to show and sell their work. This is because they need to sell items in order to afford to continue working as an artist. It also gives people the chance to see the talent of the artist.

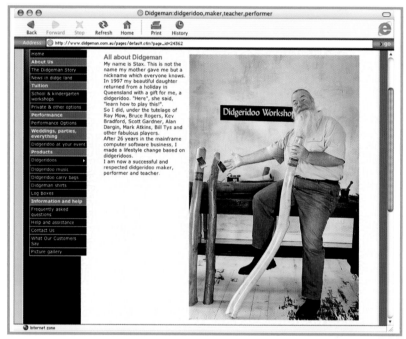

Wood artists can show their work in a studio, shop, gallery, or online. Many wood artists' groups have regular shows where artists can exhibit their works. They can also attend workshops and view the works and techniques of others.

Wood artists who make larger items need to have their own studio, as moving large items to display elsewhere can be expensive. Many traditional wood artworks can now be seen on Web sites.

◄ An online gallery in a Web site can display a large amount of artwork—more than an exhibition space can.

Making a living as a wood artist

Artists may sell their works directly from their own gallery or workshop. They can also work by commission. This happens when people seeing an artist's work want a similar piece for a particular space. They can ask the wood artist to create a piece especially for them. Some woodworkers also teach their art at schools and colleges, or to individuals.

△ This wooden bowl is an example of a production item.

Production items

Production items are all made to a similar pattern or design even though each piece of wood is different. Selling these production items means wood artists can afford to work on more individual pieces.

Wood artists who make these items can take them to markets to sell directly to the public. These can be handcrafted toys, ornaments, and bowls. They are popular because each one is an individual piece with its own character.

Wood artists' groups

There are many groups that wood artists can join. Members can be expert craftspeople or people who just enjoy woodworking as a hobby. They join to learn about woodwork arts. There are even groups that teach the ancient craft of joining wood without using modern tools.

The Wood Turning Center is based in Philadelphia and was formed in 1986. It is a not-for-profit international art gallery and resource center. The Center has the biggest collection of turned wood objects in the world, which can be seen both in the gallery and online.

Online groups

Online groups and associations can display work, share ideas, deal with issues, and even sell work over the Internet. This sharing of ideas electronically has had a major effect on woodwork artists. Techniques with wood that were being used by isolated groups can now be viewed and shared online by people all over the world.

◀ The Wood Turning Center Web site displays all kinds of turned wood artworks.

Issues for wood artists

Wood artists need to be aware of health, safety, and environmental issues that can affect their work.

Health and safety

Wood lathes, chisels, saws, and hammers can all be dangerous if used without considering health and safety. Cuts, noise, dust, and splinters are constant dangers. Safety equipment needs to be worn while using these tools. Keeping tools in good, working condition is very important. Artists must take care with varnishes, polishes, and paints which can damage skin and give off harmful fumes.

Environmental impacts

Wood artists need to consider the environmental impact of their work. Wood comes from trees and the loss of natural forests is a worldwide problem. Trees that have taken hundreds of years to grow are becoming rare. Plantation, weed species, and recycled timber are becoming more popular with wood artists for this reason.

🔺 The tools used to work with wood can be harmful if you are not aware of health and safety issues.

The Artist Speaks

"Camphor Laurel is now recognized as an Australian noxious weed. Making use of it in furniture manufacture is an environmentally friendly pursuit."
Brad McNab, timber artist

CASE STUDY
Recycling wood

In 2003, the Victorian Woodworkers Association (VWA) in Australia organized a competition called "Create with a Crate." The idea was to promote the reuse of timber that would otherwise go to waste. This is known as "eco-recycling." The challenge was to create artworks with wood from large wooden pallets used to import machinery. These are made of exotic timbers such as oak and elm.

The Artist Speaks

"The difference between the mass produced object and the piece from the designer maker is pleasure for the buyer and satisfaction for the maker."
Jane La Scala, Victorian Woodworkers Association member

◀ Wood from pallets can be reused by artists.

Fine timber used for pallets is often wasted, ending up in landfill. The competition aimed to change people's ideas about the uses of recycled wood and perhaps decrease the need for new timber. The competition produced a large variety of products.

Following on from "Create with a Crate," in 2005 the VWA started a new competition. "Woodworks" is an annual event showing the best in wood artwork. The competition is open to all artists, young and old.

◀ It is hard to believe that these artworks were made from wooden pallets.

PROJECT
Make a polished wood coaster

What you need:

- ▶ a round or square piece of wood about 4 inches (10 cm) across and 0.4 inch (1 cm) thick
- ▶ sandpaper
- ▶ a piece of felt the size of the piece of timber
- ▶ gloves
- ▶ mask
- ▶ scissors
- ▶ glue
- ▶ linseed oil
- ▶ lint-free piece of cloth

Pieces of wood cut across the grain and polished show decorative tree ring patterns. A large branch from a fruit tree, walnut tree, or gum tree would be suitable for this project. Slices from these branches can be used to make coasters to put your drinks on.

You could even try using a smooth stone to finish the surface, like the ancient Egyptians did.

Sticking felt to the bottom makes the coaster suitable for use on good furniture.

What to do:

1. Put on the gloves and mask.

2. Rub the surface with the sandpaper, rubbing in the direction of the grain.

3. Polish the surface well by rubbing repeatedly with a piece of cloth. This will take time.

4. Pour a small amount of oil onto the cloth, and rub onto the finished surface.

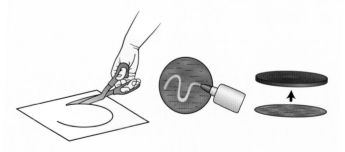

5. Cut and glue the piece of felt to the bottom.

The Artist Speaks

"I use only natural oils on my pieces. Care of the finished product involves washing in warm soapy water and then re-oiling lightly."
Steve Horton, wood artist

Wood art timeline

B.C.

500 000 Wood used to make sharpened poles

30 000 Bow and arrow used for hunting

4000+ Bow drill and lathe first used in Middle East

3500 Solid wooden wheels used on carts; saws used to cut wood

2800 Plywood used in ancient Egypt

2500 Extensive use of woodworking tools in ancient Egypt; iron saw used in Mesopotamia

600 Greeks turn wood on pole lathes

100 Romans use iron cutters in tools such as wood plane and auger

A.D.

0 Romans develop the pump drill

1300s Wheel spinning lathes developed in Europe, replacing the pole lathe

1500s Thin strip metal saw used for intricate carving of hardwoods

1600s Water driven mill saws used to cut wood

1712 Steam engine power becomes available

1789 Steam operated precision lathe invented

1830s European cabinet makers use plywood

1840s Turret lathe invented

1890s Cheap plywood furniture produced

1950s Computer operated tools introduced

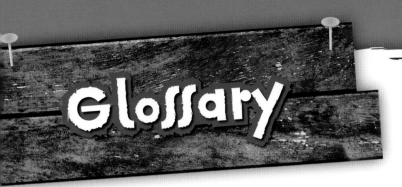

Glossary

augers tools for boring holes in wood

contemporary belonging to the present time

grain the pattern in wood formed by growth rings in the trunk or branch

laminating making something by putting one layer on top of the other

lathe a machine that rotates items to be worked by stationary tools

medium material used

planes tools for removing thin layers of a piece of wood

tongue and groove a join in two pieces of wood created by pushing one piece into a hole in the other piece

well-seasoned wood that has been cut for some time

Index